Most Favoured

David Ireland

methuen | drama

LONDON · NEW YORK · OXFORD · NEW DELHI · SYDNEY

METHUEN DRAMA

Bloomsbury Publishing Plc, 50 Bedford Square, London, WC1B 3DP, UK
Bloomsbury Publishing Inc, 1359 Broadway, New York, NY 10018, USA
Bloomsbury Publishing Ireland, 29 Earlsfort Terrace, Dublin 2,
D02 AY28, Ireland

BLOOMSBURY, METHUEN DRAMA and the Methuen
Drama logo are trademarks of Bloomsbury Publishing Plc.

First published in Great Britain 2025

Photograph by Lucas Wilson

Design by Conor Jatter

ISBN: PB: 978-1-3506-2843-4
ePDF: 978-1-3506-2845-8
eBook: 978-1-3506-2844-1

Series: Modern Plays

Typeset by Mark Heslington Ltd, Scarborough, North Yorkshire
Printed and bound in Great Britain

For product safety related questions contact
productsafety@bloomsbury.com.

To find out more about our authors and books visit
www.bloomsbury.com and sign up for our newsletters.

19th Street Productions and María Inés Olmedo Projects
in association with the Soho Theatre presents

The London Premiere

Most Favoured

by David Ireland

MOST FAVOURED

by David Ireland

Cast

Mary   **Lauren Lyle**
Mike   **Alexander Arnold**

The performance lasts approximately 45 minutes.

There will be no interval.

Director   Max Elton
Set and Costume Designer   Ceci Calf
Lighting Designer   Amy Daniels
Sound Designer   Marcus Rice
Casting Director   Rob Kelly
Stage Manager   Vivi Wei
Production Manager   Jack Boissieux/JBPM
Producer   Sarah Roy
Producer   María Inés Olmedo

Please turn your mobile phones off – the light they emit can
also be distracting.

Lauren Lyle | Mary

Lauren Lyle is a two-time BAFTA Scotland award winning actress, whose career spans film, television, and stage.

Lauren can currently be seen in the critically acclaimed BBC/Sky NZ psychological drama *The Ridge*. Shot on location in New Zealand, Lauren plays the lead role of addict Mia who is fleeing addiction and leaving a professional life in tatters; she accepts a wedding invitation from her estranged sister in New Zealand – only to find the would-be bride dead upon arrival. *The Guardian*'s Lucy Mangan described Lyle's performance as 'absolutely magnificent'. Earlier this year, Lauren reprised her role of the titular character in the second season of ITV's hit series *Karen Pirie* based on the Inspector Karen Pirie novels by Val McDermid, which follows a young detective who is put in charge of solving a forty-year-old cold case, the kidnapping of an oil heiress's son. Previously, in 2023, Lauren received two BAFTA Scotland awards, Best Actress in Television and the Audience Award for favourite Scot on Screen for her performance in season one of the show. 2025 has been a busy year as Lauren starred in the television drama series *The Bombing of Pan Am 103*, a BBC and Netflix (US) co-production. The series, also starring Connor Swindells and Peter Mullan, follows Britain's worst terrorist attack in 1988 and aired earlier this year in May. Additionally, Lauren could be seen alongside Jodie Whittaker and Aimee Lou Wood in the Netflix series *Toxic Town* playing Dani Holliday. The four-part limited series tells the real-life Corby Toxic Waste Case story that dominated headlines in the UK. The series received rave reviews when it aired in February of this year. Last year, Lauren appeared in the critically acclaimed film, *The Outrun*, which premiered as part of the 2024 Sundance Film

Festival lineup and was followed by a screening at the Berlin International Film Festival. The film – starring Saoirse Ronan, Paapa Essiedu and Stephen Dillane – was nominated in nine categories at BIFA, including 'Best British Independent Film'. Lauren is a series regular and fan favourite, playing Marsali MacKimmie Fraser in the BAFTA winning, Golden Globe and Emmy-nominated series *Outlander* alongside Caitriona Balfe and Sam Heughan. *Outlander* is a historical drama television series based on the *Outlander* novel series by Diana Gabaldon. The series follows Claire Randall, a married combat nurse from 1945 who is transported back in time to 1743, where she is immediately thrown into an unknown world in which her life is threatened. In 2021, Lyle also appeared in the BBC crime TV drama *Vigil* as Jade Antoniak, which is set on a ballistic missile submarine. Other television credits include *Broken* and *Holby City*. In 2018, audiences saw Lauren star in the film adaptation of Fiona Shaw's novel *Tell It to the Bees*, opposite Anna Paquin and Holliday Grainger, and Lily Rose Thomas' debut short film *Girls Who Drink*. Other film credits include Studio Canal's *Something in the Water* and the independent feature *Mercy Falls*. Lauren made her theatre debut in 2014 starring in the critically acclaimed production of *The Crucible* at the Old Vic Theatre. Her stage work includes several productions with the National Youth Theatre's rep program in 2015, performing in three plays during the season, *Wuthering Heights*, *Consensual* and Shakespeare's *The Merchant of Venice*.

Alexander Arnold | Mike

Born in Ashford, Kent, Alexander Arnold is best known from his roles in E4's BAFTA-winning series *Skins* and Danny Boyle's Beatles-themed musical comedy *Yesterday*, with further notebale performances in acclaimed series such as BBC's *Poldark*, and Sky Atlantic's *Save Me*.

Most recently Alex played the lead role in *Delivery Run*, as a food delivery driver caught in a deadly chase across the icy backroads of rural Minnesota. He'll be appearing in David Mackenzie's new crime heist thriller *Fuze* later next year. Arnold made his Westend debut in David Mamet's *Bitter Wheat* at the Garrick Theatre. His other theatre credits include both *Four Minutes Twelve Seconds*, and *Luna Gale* (Hampstead Theatre), *Crushed Shells and Mud* (Southwark Playhouse), *Shopping and F***ing* (Lyric Hammersmith). As well as acting, Arnold has expanded into writing and directing. His first narrative short film *11+* was shown at the San Diego Short Film Festival and had its UK premiere at the London Independent Film Festival.

David Ireland | Playwright

David was born in Belfast and trained as an actor at the Royal Conservatoire of Scotland.

His first play, *What the Animals Say*, was produced at Oran Mor, Glasgow in 2011. He was Playwright-in-Residence at the Lyric Theatre, Belfast in 2012. He went on to win the Meyer Whitworth Award in 2012 for his second play, *Everything Between Us*, produced by Tinderbox Theatre Company in Belfast. In 2016 *Cyprus Avenue*, featuring Stephen Rea, opened at the Abbey Theatre, Dublin before transferring to the Royal Court, London and then on to the Public Theatre, New York. It won the *Irish Times* Award for Best New Play and the James Tait Black Award in 2017. In 2018, *Ulster American* was produced at the Traverse Theatre as part of the Edinburgh Fringe. It won a *Scotsman* Fringe First and the Critics Award for Theatre in Scotland for Best New Play. Ulster American was revived by Second Half Productions at the Riverside Studios, London in 2023 featuring Woody Harrelson, Andy Serkis and Louisa Harland. In 2024, *The Fifth Step* was produced by National Theatre of Scotland for a short run before transferring to @sohoplace starring Martin Freeman and Jack Lowden produced by Playful Productions and Neal Street. His other plays include *Not Now* (Oran Mor & Finborough Theatre), *Sadie* (Lyric, Belfast) *Yes So I Said Yes* (Ransom Productions, Belfast & Finborough Theatre), *The End of Hope* (Oran Mor & Soho Theatre) and *Can't Forget About You* (Lyric, Belfast). His first TV series, *The Lovers*, was broadcast on Sky Atlantic in 2023. His latest TV series, *Cold Water*, featuring Andrew Lincoln, was broadcast on ITV in September 2025.

As an actor, he is best known for playing Clare's Dad in *Derry Girls*.

Max Elton | Director

Max Elton is a director, dramaturg and writer. He is currently Associate Director (Literary) at Soho Theatre. His production of *Not Now* by David Ireland (Finborough Theatre, Lyric Belfast) was listed as #6 in *The Observer*'s Plays of 2022 and he was nominated for Broadway World's Director of the Year for the same production. Other previous full productions include *Yes So I Said Yes* and *The Melting Pot* (Finborough Theatre), *The End of Hope* (Orange Tree/Soho Theatre) which was nominated for Best New Play at the Off West End Awards and *Big Brother Blitzkrieg* (King's Head Theatre), which he also wrote. Associate work includes *Sheppey* (Orange Tree) and *Madame Rubinstein* (Park

Theatre). In 2023, Max was invited to take part in the National Theatre's Directors' Course.

Ceci Calf | Set and Costume Designer

Ceci is a set and costume designer based in London, with experience working across the UK and Europe in Theatre, Opera, and Dance. Recent credits include: *Emma* (Theatre Royal Bath/UK Tour), *Comedy of Errors* (Shakespeare Theatre Company, Washington), *Don Giovanni, The Barber of Seville* (Waterperry Festival Opera), *HIR* starring Felicity Huffman, *Our Cosmic Dust* (Park Theatre), *Stiletto: The Musical* (Charing Cross Theatre), *Farm Hall* (Jermyn Street/ Theatre Royal Bath/UK Tour/West End), *Autobiography of a Cad, Much Ado About Nothing, Othello* (Watermill Theatre, Newbury), *A Christmas Carol* (Opera Holland Park/ Concert), *The Ritual Slaughter of Gorge Mastromas, A Skull In Connemara* (Dailes Theatre, Riga, Latvia), *Under The Black Rock* (Arcola), *Warrior Queens* (Sadler's Wells), *Waiting For Anya* (Barn Theatre), *Yes So I Said Yes* (Winner of Standing Ovation Award: Best Production) Associate credits: *Macbeth* starring Ralph Fiennes and *Anything Is Possible If You Think About It Hard Enough* (Southwark Playhouse).

Amy Daniels | Lighting Designer

Amy (she/her) is a London-based freelance lighting designer, with occasional stints as a technical stage manager. A lover of theatre since she can remember, she studied English Literature at the University of Sussex, then fell in love with all things production during a year abroad at Stony Brook University in New York. She was the technical manager at Camden People's Theatre from August 2018 until September 2022, during which time she focused her practice from technical management towards production lighting and lighting design. She works on a wide range of performance, with an emphasis on the political, the playful and the pondering.

Marcus Rice | Sound Designer

Marcus Rice, aka Hungry Tapes, is a sound designer and composer from south London working across theatre, animation, film and podcast. Recent credits and collaborators include Blinkink, BBC, Soho Theatre Walthamstow and Sam Campbell, and big brands such as Tate, RSPCA, Muji and McDonald's.

Rob Kelly | Casting Director

Rob Kelly is a London-based Casting Director dedicated to discovering and championing exceptional talent. With a background in performance, he has helped launch the careers of award-winning actors, including recent BAFTA Rising Stars. Passionate about diversity and authenticity, Rob is committed to amplifying working-class voices, LGBTQ+ talent, and actors from underrepresented backgrounds. Television credits include *A Knock at The Door, Never Too Late, Wild, The Village Idiot* and *The Quiet Hour* (Channel 5), *Geek Girl* (Netflix), *Curfew* (Paramount+), *Phoenix Rise* (BBC Three), *Free Rein* (Netflix), *Gangsta Granny Strikes Again* (BBC), *The Drowning* (Netflix), *Pandora* (The CW), *Whitstable Pearl* (AMC), *Dodger* (BBC), *Hard Cell* (Netflix), *Flowers in the Attic: The Origin* (Paramount+), *Bulletproof* (Sky), *The Royals* (Lionsgate), *The Athena* (Amazon/Sky), *Almost Never* (BBC), *The A List* (Netflix), *Malory Towers* (BBC), *Jamie Johnson* (BBC), *Hank Zipzer* (BBC), *California Dreaming* (Viacom), *Will Vs the Future* (Amazon), *The Midnight Gang* (BBC), *Creeped Out* (Netflix), *The Lodge* (Disney) and *Demon Headmaster* (BBC). Film credits include *Fing* (Sky), *How to Date Billy Walsh* (Amazon), *Robin and the Hoods* (Sky), *Something in the Water* (StudioCanal), *This Is Christmas* (Sky), *Matriarch* (Hulu), *Twist* (Sky/Epix), *Her Pen Pal* (Hallmark), *Family Pictures* (Sony), *Very Valentine* (Lifetime), *Harry & Meghan: Becoming Royal* (A&E), *Bixler High Private Eye* (Nickelodeon), *Harry & Meghan: A Royal Romance* (A&E) and *Descendants 2* (Disney). Theatre credits include *Hadestown* (West End), *Most Favoured*

(Soho Theatre), *This Bitter Earth* (Soho Theatre), *Driving Miss Daisy* (York Theatre Royal), *Country Music* (Omnibus Theatre), *Passion* (Hope Mill Theatre), *Stalled: The Musical* (King's Head) and *Faygele* (Marylebone Theatre). Upcoming projects include the feature films *Libby and Joan*, *Gypsy Queen* and *Best Mary Wins*, as well as *Little Shop of Horrors* (Liverpool Empire, Hope Mill) and Boy George's *Taboo*, directed by Michael Longhurst.

Vivi Wei | Stage Manager

Vivi Wei is a technical and stage manager, performer and singer from China. Her roles in stage management, acting, singing,and workshop facilitation span the UK and China, but her true passion lies in multi-disciplinary approaches, particularly in migrant theatre, utilizing storytelling to address socio-political issues and amplify marginalized voices. Her work includes *The Dao of Unrepresentative British Chinese Experience* (Kakilang, Soho Theatre), *Cinderella* (Brixton House), *Project Atom Boi* (Camden People's Theatre, Artist Choice Award in Vault festival), *Lessons on Revolution* (Jermyn Street Theatre), *Useless* (Brixton House), *Dreamaker Theatre Festival* (Changjiang Theatre, Shanghai). Work with young people includes Assembly Festival (Company Three) and KATZENMUSIK (London Youth Theatre).

Jack Boissieux/JBPM | Production Management

JBPM is a production management company, working across theatre, opera, dance, musicals and events. They have worked on a range of projects including national and international touring productions, West End musicals and immersive/site specific theatre.

Recent and current credits include: *The Choir Of Man* (West End, European and International Touring); *Bluey's Big Play* (European and International Touring); *Weather Girl* (Soho Theatre and St Anne's Warehouse); *Shedinburgh; How To Win*

Against History (Bristol Old Vic); *OHIO* (National Tour); *The Book Thief* (Prince of Wales); *ROAM* (Shaftesbury Theatre); *Garry Starr Classic Penguins* (Soho Theatre, Edinburgh and West End); *Waterperry Opera Festival 2021–2024*; *Pied Piper* (National Touring); *The Ancient Oak Of Baldor* (National Touring); *A Very Naughty Christmas* (Southwark Playhouse, Elephant); *Wilko* (Queen's Theatre Hornchurch); *Lay Down Your Burdens* (Barbican and National Touring); *Lavender, Hyacinth, Violet, Yew* (Bush Theatre); *Four Play* (King's Head Theatre); *Echo* (King's Head Theatre); *Lost Lending Library* and *A Curious Quest* (Punchdrunk); *Maddie Moate's Very Curious Christmas* (Apollo Theatre and Garrick Theatre).

Sarah Roy | Producer & General Manager

Sarah Roy trained and worked as an actor in New York before moving back to the UK and founding 19th Street Productions. She produced and performed the critically acclaimed one woman show, *Catherine And Anita*, (Edinburgh Fringe Festival (Assembly Rooms) and Kings Head Theatre). The script was then adapted into the feature film, *Zebra Girl*, which she produced, co-wrote and starred in alongside Tom Cullen and Jade Anouka. *Zebra Girl* was nominated for Best Thriller at the National Film Awards 2021. Sarah then produced *Yes So I Said Yes* by David Ireland to rave reviews, winning Best Production at the London Pub Theatre Awards 2021. She followed this with a production of *Not Now*, also by David Ireland (both at the Finborough Theatre). *Not Now* was included in *The Observer*'s Top 10 shows of 2022.

Sarah was Associate Producer of the Tony Award-winning musical *A Strange Loop* at The Barbican in 2023.

In 2025, Sarah produced the London Premiere of the four-star play *The Problem With The Seventh Year* by *Evening Standard* Award-nominated writer Nicholas Pierpan at the White Bear Theatre.

She is currently producing the short film, *Still Life*, written by Kate Radcliffe and directed by Sophie King (*Buffering, Disability Benefits*) starring Ophelia Lovibond and Jacob Anderson.

Sarah is a recipient of the Stage One bursary.

www.19thstreetproductions.com | @19thstreetproductions

María Inés Olmedo | Producer & General Manager

María Inés is a Mexican, London-based producer and theatre-maker with an MFA in Advanced Theatre Practice from the Royal Central School of Speech and Drama. With over a decade of international experience in theatre, opera, and film, she has collaborated on more than 30 productions across the UK and Mexico.

West End credits include:

Co-Producer of *A Strange Loop* (Barbican, 2023).

Associate Producer of *Shifters* (Duke of York's, 2025), *A Mirror* (Trafalgar, 2023), and *Best of Enemies* (Noël Coward, 2022).

In 2022, María Inés was selected as a Stage One Trainee Producer at Playful Productions, where she worked on *Wicked* (Apollo Victoria), *Walking With Ghosts* (Lyric), and *The Unfriend* (Criterion).

Other projects include:

Producing and General Managing *A Fantastic Bohemian* (Arcola Theatre, 2018), a sold-out and four-star immersive opera, which she also adapted and directed. *Invisibles* (Vault Festival, 2020), featured in Lyn Gardner's and London *Evening Standard*'s top 10 shows to watch. *Terrifying Women: Gutted* (Omnibus Theatre, 2024), written by Olivier Award-winning playwright Morgan Lloyd Malcolm, Abi Zakarian and Sampira, and Co-Producer of *Invasive Species* (King's Head Theatre, 2025).

Before founding MIO Projects in London, María Inés worked as Assistant Director at Birmingham Opera Company, the Royal Opera House, and English National Opera (2019). In Mexico, she has developed and produced more than 20 acclaimed theatre, musical, and opera productions since 2012, collaborating with Grammy Award-winning, Oscar-nominated, and emerging artists.

MIO's mission is to inspire audiences worldwide through thought-provoking, heart-warming, and soul-awakening stories that have a universal resonance with today's world.

María Inés is a beneficiary of the UK's Tier 1 Exceptional Talent Visa, a Stage One Bursary recipient, and an Associate Member of SOLT.

www.mioprojects.com.mx | @mioprojects

Production Credits:

General Managers	María Inés Olmedo
	Sarah Roy
Production Management Assistants	Emma Vize/JBPM
	Ida Pontoppidan/JBPM
Production Finance Consultant	Akos Koranteg
Press Representative	Bread and Butter PR
Social Media Manager	Eleni Cashell
Media Ads Campaign	Cousins
Artwork Photographer	Lucas Wilson

Production Acknowledgements:

Stage One; Louise Goodman, Joe Smith, Olivia Polglase, Abbi Roberts, Heather Macinnes. Aron Rollin, Vivek Shukla, Lil Lambey, Kat Pierce, Alan Stacey. To all the friends and family of 19th Street Productions and María Inés Olmedo Projects and to all our wonderful investors and supporters who helped make this production happen.

About Soho Theatre

Soho Theatre is London's most vibrant producer of new theatre, comedy and cabaret. A charity and social enterprise, we're driven by a passion for working with bold stories and distinctive artists, connecting them with audiences in original style and creating memorable nights out.

From our early roots in the radical 1970s Soho Poly, we've grown – *and grown* – from a tiny fringe space into a widely influential cultural organisation operating across our four London performance spaces; through international touring and collaborations with India and elsewhere; as festival regulars from Edinburgh Festival Fringe to Melbourne International Comedy; and filming shows and creating our own digital work seen across social platforms and inflight.

Alongside working with some of the most exciting theatre-makers and comedians in the world, we also nurture the next generation of artists through a thriving range of artist and talent development programmes, artists under commission and in development, and two new writing awards including UK's longest established playwriting prize, the Verity Bargate Award.

In 2025 we're celebrating 25 years at our central London venue Soho Theatre – described by Phoebe Waller-Bridge as the 'the mothership of new artists', Ryan Calais Cameron as 'a major launchpad' and Bryony Kimmings as 'an extraordinary place for people whose work is genre pushing' – whilst opening London's newest venue, the 'jaw-dropping 1,000 seat new theatre' (*Time Out*), Soho Theatre Walthamstow in May 2025.

sohotheatre.com I @sohotheatre I @sohotheatreindia

Audience Team Soho Mischa Alexander, Erol Arguden, Brenton Arrendell, Farah Ashraf, Aiyana Bartlett, Ellie Bibby, Auriella Campolina, Becca Carr, Geri Carr, Bronya Doyle, Ben Falacci, Gabriel Harris, Oscar Holloway, Andrew Houghton, Hana Jennings, Lee King-Brown, Tilly Marples, Faith Martin, Kit Miles, Benji Morris, Paul Murphy, Fiona Oakley, Jack Parry, Janisha Perera, Jesse Phillippi, Rosie Revan, Fash Rokey, Alexis Sakellaris, Genevieve Sabherwal, Genevieve Sinha, Johnie Spillane, Sami Sumaria, Dylan Sweet, Abby Timms, Lauren Tranter, Jade Warner-Clayton, Joanne Williams, Eilis Woods.

Soho Theatre Bar Rishay Naidoo, Damian Regan, Cazz Regan, MD Ridoy Khan, Sneha Adhikari, Simon Berry, Megan Chloe Bowles, Emma Brunet Campain de Bony de Lavergne, Sofia Dixon, Lauryn Louise Giovanni, Bibin Gopi, Madeleine Hilton, Abin Marson, Zara Mehrban, Tayafur Rahman, Caleb Seed, Sian Clare Walsh, Chi Whon Won, Zaza Wright

The Goldsmiths' Company
Harold Hyam Wingate Foundation
Hyde Park Place Estate Charity
The Ian Mactaggart Trust
The Idlewild Trust
The John Thaw Foundation
John Lyon's Charity
KKL Charity
The Kobler Trust
Lara Atkin Charitable Foundation
The Leche Trust
The Mackintosh Foundation
Mohamed S. Farsi Foundation
#My Westminster Fund
Noel Coward Foundation
The Peggy Ramsay Foundation
The Rose Foundation
The Royal Victoria Hall Foundation
Santander Foundation
Schroder Charity Trust
The St James's Piccadilly Charity
Tallow Chandlers Benevolent Fund
The Teale Charitable Trust
The Thistle Trust
Unity Theatre Charitable Trust

Soho Theatre Performance Friends
Ali Braithwaite
Anna Bordon
Amanda Rajkumar
Helen Evans
Bhags Sharma
Rich Thorpe
Chris Thomas
Gary Wilder

Soho Theatre Playwright Friends
Maital Dar
Mrs Emily Fletcher

Liam Goddard
Andrew Lucas
Emma Whitting

Smoking is not permitted in the auditorium and the use of cameras and recording equipment is strictly prohibited.

**STAGE
ONE**

The producers of MOST FAVOURED wish to acknowledge financial support from Stage One, a registered charity that invests in new commercial productions. Stage One supports new UK theatre producers and productions and is committed to securing the future of commercial theatre through educational and investment schemes. Stage One would like to thank all producers, theatre owners and productions that voluntarily contribute to the levy which support this investment. For further information please visit www.stageone.uk.com.

Stage One is the operating name of the Theatre Investment Fund Ltd, a registered charity no.271349

Most Favoured was originally staged as a reading at the Traverse during the 2012 Edinburgh Fringe as part of their "Dream Plays" season starring Gabriel Quigley and Jordan McCurrach. It then became a co-production between the Traverse and Play Pie Pint/Oran Mor in March 2013 with Gabriel Quigley and Richard Rankin.

The London Premiere was first produced by 19th Street Productions and María Inés Olmedo Projects in association with the Soho Theatre. It was first presented at the Soho Theatre on Thursday 11 December 2025.

Most Favoured

for Elijah

Characters

Mike, *American, twenty to thirty*
Mary, *Scottish, thirty to forty*

A room in a Travelodge near Haymarket Station, Edinburgh. It's early morning. **Mike**, *an attractive young man in boxer shorts, sits at the top of a bed devouring a huge bucket of Kentucky Fried Chicken. He's American.* **Mary** *enters from the bathroom. She's just had a shower and wears only a towel. She's in her late thirties, from Glasgow. She opens the curtains and the sun shines in. She sits at the end of the bed.*

Mary Oh my God. What a morning.

Mike Mm.

Mary Ohhhh . . .

Mike Mmm.

Mary Oh hoh hoh . . . What a morning.

Mike Mmmmm.

Mary And what a night! Ho ho! What a night!

Mike Yes. It was.

Mary Wasn't it?

Mike It was something else.

Mary It was . . . oh aye . . .

Mike Mm. mmmm.

Mary Do you mind me telling you that last night was incredible?

Mike No. I do not.

Mary It doesn't feel weird or clingy or whatever else to say that to you?

Mike No. Not at all.

Mary I've never felt like this before. Don't take that the wrong way, I'm not being –

Mike I understand.

Mary   I mean I'm not wanting to marry you or anything!

Mike   Ha hah.

Mary   But I can honestly say . . . I've never 'felt' like 'this' before.

Mike   Yeah I know what you mean.

Mary   Do you?

Mike   I feel exactly the same about this chicken.

Mary   What?

Mike   The way you feel about last night? That's how I feel about this chicken.

I've never felt this way about chicken before. This is the best chicken I've ever had in my life.

Mary   It's KFC.

Mike   It's beautiful.

Mary   You know it's just KFC, don't you?

Mike   What's KFC?

Mary   That is.

Mike   But what is KFC?

Mary   What do you mean?

Mike   What is it?

Mary   Kentucky Fried Chicken.

Mike   What's that?

Mary   What are you talking about?

Mike   What's Kentucky Fried Chicken?

Mary   'What's Kentucky Fried Chicken?'

Mike   Yeah what is it? I never heard of it.

Mary   Are you serious?

Mike   Yeah.

Mary   Where did you say you were from again?

Mike   Indiana.

Mary   You're from Indiana and you've never heard of Kentucky Fried Chicken?

Mike   Nope.

Mary   How can that be? That's not possible. How is that possible?

Mike   I'm from a very small town.

Mary   Have you heard of McDonald's?

Mike   No.

Mary   Burger King?

Mike (*shaking his head*)   Uh-uh.

Mary   Pizza Hut?

Mike   I've never heard of any of these places. We don't have this kind of food in the States. Believe me, if we had this in the States, I'd be eating it all the time.

Mary   It's called 'Kentucky'! '*Kentucky* Fried Chicken'!

Mike   It's probably a European company using the American name to sell stuff.

Mary   No I really don't think so. No I find this very hard to believe.

Mike   I don't know what else to tell you, I never heard of it before.

Mary   No I think you're having some kind of a joke at my expense.

Mike   No no. That's not what I'm doing. Absolutely not.

Mary   But how could . . .?

Actually maybe you're right, maybe they don't have Kentucky Fried Chicken in America . . .

No! They must have! They must have it over there!

Mike   Is it really such a big deal?

Mary   Yes! This is impossible! It's impossible that you have never heard of Kentucky Fried Chicken.

Mike   Nothing is impossible.

His devouring becomes orgasmic now, bestial.

Awwww . . . I can't get enough of it . . . ohhhhhh . . . it's . . . mmmmmmmmmmmmmmmmmmmmm . . .

He sees her staring at him.

Do you want some?

Mary   No.

Mike   Are you sure? It's amazing.

Mary   No I don't like Kentucky Fried Chicken.

Mike   This? You don't like this?

Mary   No.

Mike   How could you not like this?

Mary   Because it's disgusting.

Mike   Are you kidding? This chicken is . . .

Mary   Revolting?

Mike   Exemplary! It's *exemplary*!

Mary   It's very unhealthy. Especially for breakfast.

Mike   Really? It's unhealthy?

Mary   It's *very* unhealthy. And I'm from Glasgow. If I know about anything, it's unhealthy breakfasts.

He examines the chicken leg he's eating, mournfully.

Mike   I feel betrayed now.

He shrugs and continues eating anyway.

Mary   We were talking about uhm . . .

Mike   Last night?

Mary   Did you like it?

Mike   Sure. It was great.

Mary   Really? Do you really think so? Or are you just saying that?

Mike   No, I enjoyed it. Really. It was excellent.

Mary   Wasn't it though? I mean, really, wasn't it?

Mike   It was pretty terrific.

Mary   It was absolutely incredible!

I can't stop thinking about it!

I can't stop thinking about it . . .

She is lost in thought. **Mike** *keeps eating the chicken.*

Mary   I'm trying to right now but I literally cannot stop thinking about it!

I felt like, I felt . . .

Mike   Oh, THANK YOU, GOD!

Mary   What?

Mike   There's fries in here too!

This is turning out to be the best morning of my entire life!

He eats a huge handful of fries, stuffing them into his mouth.

Ugh.

He spits them out.

Mary   Do you not like them?

Still with some fries in his mouth, he shakes his head no.

Mike   Mm-mm.

How can the chicken be so good but the fries so bad?

Mary   That's KFC for you.

Do you mind if we keep talking about last night? I know you're like, really into the chicken and that, but can we talk about last night? And stop talking about the chicken?

Mike   Sure. Ok.

Mary   Can you close your eyes as well?

Mike   Why?

Mary   Or turn around?

Mike   Why?

Mary   I want to put my clothes on.

Mike   You're putting your – ok.

Mary   Do you mind?

Mike   I just – I thought you might want to do it again.

Mary   Oh. Well, I have to say I hadn't really considered that possibility.

Mike   No?

Mary   No. I don't like morning sex. I know men all love it, but I can't stand it, it's like uuuugh bad breath and messy hair and horrible smells and . . . aw no. No no no.

Mike   That's cool.

Mary   Not for me. No no no. No.

Mike   Ok.

Mary   Aw!

Mike   What?

Mary   I feel bad now!

Mike   It's cool.

Mary   I feel bad for rejecting you!

Mike   Don't feel bad.

Mary   I'm so sorry!

Mike   Hey it's ok.

Mary   I'm not good at saying no to people. I feel terrible now!

Mike   No, hey, look, hey. It's fine, it's, really it's fine. I just thought, you know, you keep saying how good it was last night.

Mary   It was!

Mike   So I assumed you'd be interested in . . .

Mary   Hmm.

Mike   *'continuez la droite'.*

Mary   What?

Mike   Nothing, it's just –

Mary   Ok.

Mike   I was speaking French. Bit of French.

Mary   Ah.

Mike   I'm in Europe.

Mary   Look. It was perfect. Last night. It was perfect. And I want that to be my memory . . . of you.

Mike   That's cool.

Mary   Is it really?

Mike   Yeah, yeah. Sure.

Mary   So . . .?

Mike   What?

Mary   Do you mind turning around?

Mike   Yep. Sure.

He turns around.

She takes off her towel and puts her clothes on.

Mary   I'm . . . you can . . . hello?

He turns back round.

Thank you.

Mike   Are we done talking about last night now?

Mary   No. Why?

Mike   Ok.

Mary   Are you bored talking about it?

Mike   No, no. I just wanted to get back to talking about the chicken. But we can keep talking about last night. If you want.

Mary   If you don't mind.

Mike   Go ahead.

Mary   Ok. Now. There is something else I need to address. If that's ok.

Mike   Yeah yeah.

Mike   I know this was a one-night thing. I said that last night, didn't I?

Mike   Yes you did.

Mary   That I'm not looking for anything special, for anything permanent.

Mike   Yeah sure.

Mary   So I know that when I say what I'm about to say you won't take this the wrong way? And if I didn't say this, if I didn't address this now, it would feel weird.

Mike   What is it?

Mary   And I also want to tell you that – so that you don't assume after I tell you what I'm about to tell you that I'm sort of stalker, that I'm some sort of crazy psycho bitch who's getting possessive and neurotic over what is essentially a 'one-night stand' – I should also tell you that I have done this a lot these past eight months. A *lot*. With many different men. And when I say a lot, I mean *a lot. A lot.*

Mike   Ok. What's a lot?

Mary   *A lot.* That's all you need to know. *A lot.*

Mike   Ok.

Mary   With many different men.

Mike   Ok. Cool.

Mary   But last night, when we did it. When you and I . . .

I . . .

I just want you to know that for the first time in my life I felt loved.

I know for you it might have been just a casual . . .

Mike   No.

Mary   But for me, it was love. It felt like love. Or the closest I've ever come to love. And I wanted to say thank you. For that.

And that's it.

Mike   Ok.

Mary   Now I'm sorry if that was a weird thing to have to hear.

Mike   No.

Mary   Cos I know a lot of guys would feel very weird if some lassie they didnae know said something like that to them the morning after a one-night stand.

Mike   It's not weird.

Mary   Some 'random chick'. Some '*burd*'.

Mike   You're not random. None of this is random.

Mary   Yeah well . . . what does that mean?

Mike   Nothing.

Mary   Yeah. Nothing.

Well.

I'm going to go now.

Mike   Ok.

Mary   It was lovely meeting you. Mike.

Mike   You too. Mary.

Mary   Have a nice . . .

Mike   Yes. You too.

She bends down to kiss him on the cheek, awkwardly. She is nearly out the door when . . .

Oh no! Mary!

Mary   Yes?

Mike   There's something I need to ask you.

Mary   Yes?

Mike   It's about the chicken.

Mary   The chicken?

Mike   Can I get this in London? I'm going to London after Edinburgh. Do they have this 'Kentucky Fried Chicken' place in London too? Or is it only in Scotland?

Mary   Yes, they have Kentucky Fried Chicken in London.

Mike   Where?

Mary   Everywhere.

Mike   So it won't be a problem finding one?

Mary   I shouldn't think so.

Mike   Ok. That's a relief.

Mary   Hmmm.

Mike   Phew!

Mary   Ok then. Bye.

She stops at the door.

She goes back and sits on the bed.

She bows her head and puts her hand on her forehead.

Mike   What's wrong?

Mary   I can't leave.

Mike   Oh. Ok.

Why not?

Mary   There's something else I need to tell you.

Mike   Ok. What is it . . . this time?

Mary   Alright, this is big. This is a big thing.

Mike   Ok.

Mary   The only reason I'm telling you this –

Mike   What are you telling me?

Mary   Let me get to it in my own time.

I'm telling you this because of . . . well, because of how you made me feel last night . . . that you made me feel . . . you know . . .

Mike   Yes, loved. You said.

Mary   Yes. Exactly, yes.

So because of this, I have something important to tell you. And it might freak you out.

Mike   Ok.

Mary   Could you put the bucket of chicken down please?

He does so.

Remember I told you I did this a lot this year?

Mike   Yeah of course.

Mary   With many different men. Do you remember I said that?

Mike   Yeah it was only like two minutes ago. Of course I remember.

Mary   January of this year, I made a resolution I would try to do it with as many men as I possibly could. Now I don't mean like gangbangs or anything.

Mike   Right.

Mary   Nothing weird. Just like one-on-one normal straightforward –

Now – as you can see I'm getting on a bit in the age department.

Mike   No.

Mary   Now you don't need to be –

Mike   I think you look good.

Mary   This isn't the time to be – you don't have to be –

Mike   I think you look great.

Mary   Flattering or complimentary.

Mike   I really do think you look fantastic though. You're a very sexy woman.

Mary   Come on! Well, thank you. 'A very sexy woman'! Well, thank you. But no.

I'm turning forty this year.

Mike   That actually surprises me.

Mary   And I want a baby.

Mike   … . ok . . .?

Mary   Last night I told you we didn't have to use protection because I was on the pill.

Mike   Yes and I was very relieved because, as I told you, I hate wearing condoms.

Mary   Well. I lied to you, Mike. Yes.

I'm not on the pill. I never have been.

For the past eight months, night after night I have been having sex with an array of random strangers in an attempt to impregnate myself and so have a baby before I turn forty-one.

I live in Glasgow, as you know. That's another city here in Scotland, quite nearby. It's a big city and I've had sex with many of the men there. But I thought . . . well, I saw the Edinburgh Festival was on, and I don't normally come through to Edinburgh when the Festival's on because, well, it's just so busy, and the train through is so busy and I don't like Edinburgh at the best of times anyway. But I thought. Well, Edinburgh Festival. Lots of different men from all over the world. Tourists. Actors. Stand-up comedians. It makes sense that they'd be getting drunk and looking for casual sex. So I thought – well, I might meet somebody different, somebody with a bit of glamour, you know, good genes, and it feels like I've had sex with every man in Glasgow I would want to have sex with. And believe me Glasgow men are not renowned for their glamour or their good genes. So it made sense to come through and meet someone – well, someone like you. Mike. That makes sense doesn't it? You can see it makes sense, yes?

Now I realise this is bad. That this kind of behaviour is at the very least questionable, if not completely immoral, not to say dangerous.

But I really want a baby. I feel like I am meant to be a mother. That that is what I am supposed to be in life.

I don't normally tell the men I sleep with this information.

I don't want the baby to have a father. I'm happy to raise my baby alone. In fact, that's what I want.

But – I just want to tell you that if I do get pregnant. And if the baby I have turns out to be from this particular encounter. If the baby is yours, Mike, is what I'm saying . . . then I'm happy for you to take as active a part as you like in the baby's life. Or not. You can be a father to her. Or him. Or not.

It's up to you.

And that's because of last night. And how you made me feel. And I'm very glad I met you. And had that experience.

And . . . that's all.

Mike *just nods. He has no idea what to say.*

Mary   Now I know that's a lot to take in.

And you must think I'm . . .

Nuts . . .

But . . .

Are you feeling ok?

Mike   Uh . . . yeah . . .

Yeah yeah yeah.

He picks up his bucket of chicken and starts eating it again.

Thanks for telling me. I appreciate it.

Mary   Is there anything you want to know?

Mike   Um . . . no.

Mary   No?

Mike   No.

Mary   No?

Mike   No. That all sounds good. I'm happy. Whatever.

Mary   Right. Are you sure you're happy?

Mike   Yeah yeah.

Mary   Cos you don't sound happy.

Mike   I am. Really I am.

Mary   Ok.

Mike   I wish I could get the TV to work.

She sits thinking. **Mike** *keeps eating.*

Mary   I have to tell you I'm quite surprised by your reaction, Mike.

Mike   Yeah?

Mary   Yeah. I mean, most men, most men if they were told something like that would completely freak out.

Mike   Would they?

Mary   Yeah. I think so. Yeah I'd say so.

Mike   Well, I guess I'm not most men.

Mary   It genuinely doesn't bother you what I've just said?

Mike   Not really.

Well, the chances are you're not pregnant, right? I mean not with me. If you've been sleeping with all these men, it's unlikely that my 'goo' will be the one to connect with your – you know? Whatever it's called.

Mary   Egg.

Mike   Yeah, your . . . is it really called an 'egg'?

Mary   Yes.

Mike   Wow.   So if you get pregnant – congratulations! Good luck with it! If it's mine, great. Have fun with it. With my blessing. It's all good.

Mary   Right. Ok. Well, that's . . . I see . . .

Mike   So . . . are we done here? If you want to leave it's fine. Don't feel you have to stay.

Mary   Ahm . . . yeah. Yeah. Yeah . . .

No. No. This . . . doesn't feel right.

Mike   Ok.

Mary   Something about this whole situation doesn't feel right.

Mike   Ok.

Mary   Shouldn't you be angry or something?

Mike   Should I?

Mary   Yes! I lied to you!

Mike   So what? Human beings lie all the time.

Mary   But I've possibly made you a father against your will. I could be carrying your child, Mike!

Mike   Yeah that's great.

Mary   Great?

Mike   I love kids. Great! Hooray!

Mary   So . . . Do you want to be involved? If you are the father?

Mike   Yeah. No. Maybe. Whatever.

Mary   Well, do you or don't you?

Mike   Let's see.

Mary   Your reaction to all this is very, very strange.

Mike   I don't think so.

Mary   No it is. You're a very, very strange man.

Mike   I don't think I'm being strange at all

Mary   Do you fancy me?

Mike   What? Like what does that . . .?

Mary   Do you have, like, some sort of weird crush on me?

Mike   Ah . . . not that I . . . I don't . . .

Mary   Are you in love with me?

Mike   No! Oh my God, no!

Mary   Really?

Mike   Of course not, I only met you last night.

Mary   Because this is all very odd.

Mike   I don't think there's anything odd about this at all. Are you on socialist media?

Mary   What's socialist media?

Mike   Not uhm . . . what's it . . . *social* media?

Mary   . . . Yes.

Mike   Well, how about, if, after the baby's born, if it looks anything like me, why don't you get in touch with me via 'social media' and we can . . . you know . . . figure something out?

Mary   'Social media'?

Mike   Yeah? That's what it's called, right?

Mary   What – what is this? What is going on here?

Mike   I don't know what you mean.

Mary   Are you just daft? Or am I daft?

Mike   I don't know what that word means.

Mary   Or am I missing something here? I feel like there is something I am not being told? That you, Mike, that you are keeping something from me?

Mike   No.

Mary   What is it? Tell me what it is!

Mike   Uh . . .

Mary   There is something isn't there?

Mike   Ah . . . No?

Mary   No there is. I can see there is. I can tell.

Mike   Well, there isn't. So . . . goodbye.

He offers her his hand to shake.

Mary   No. No I'm not going anywhere till you tell me what's going on.

Mike   Nothing's going on!

Mary   Something's going on! Let me tell you I have a very good instinct for this kind of thing.

Mike   What kind of thing? There is no thing!

Mary   I have an instinct for when someone is concealing something from me. It's one of the qualities which makes me a natural mother. You have something to tell me, don't you?

Mike   No!

Mary   You do! I know you do!

Mike   How would you know that? How could you know?

Mary   I can tell. Things like this, I can tell!

Mike   Well, there's nothing to tell. So –

He shouts at her, trying to be authoritative but failing.

GO! GET OUT OF HERE! LEAVE!

Mary   I'm not leaving here till you tell me whatever it is you don't want to tell me.

Mike *lets out a giant aggravated sigh, almost a roar.*

Mike   Awwwwwwwwwwww.

Oh God.

God God God.

This is typical. This is so . . .

Alright. Alright.

I'll tell you but after I tell you you have to promise you'll go and leave me alone. Ok?

Mary   What is it?

Mike   Do you promise after I tell you this you'll go away?

Mary   Just tell me!

Mike   Only if you promise you'll leave me alone?

Mary   How can I promise something like that without knowing what you're going to tell me?

Mike   Fine then I won't tell you.

Mary   Then I won't leave!

Mike   Fine then I'll leave.

Mary   Well, I'll follow you.

Mike   Well, I'll run away.

Mary   Well, I'll chase after you.

Mike   Well, I'll run faster!

Mary   Alright, look! Fine! I promise I'll leave you alone after you tell me.

Mike   You'll leave here and let me be?

Mary   Yes. What is it?

Mike   Sit down.

Mary   Why?

Mike   You're going to be shocked when I tell you what I have to tell you so I insist you sit down.

Mary   Why am I going to be shocked?

Mike   Just sit!

She sits.

You are pregnant.

Mary   What?

Mike   You are pregnant. Last night, I impregnated you.

Mary   What are you talking about?

Mike   Alright, alright.

Mary   How could you know?

Mike   Alright, alright.

Mary   What are you saying?

Mike   This is a big deal. Ok? Remember you said to me that what you said to me was a big deal? Well, that wasn't a big deal. What I'm about to tell you now is really a big deal. Like the biggest deal imaginable.

Mary   It can't be that big a deal.

Mike   Oh it is. It is.

Mary   Whatever it is it can't be bigger than what I told you.

Mike   Oh it is. It is.

Mary   Well . . . what then?

Mike   You'll probably think I'm lying and you'll experience an enormous amount of confusion.

Mary   For God's sake, what is it? Just tell me!

Mike   There's a very good reason I've never heard of this chicken place, this 'Kentucky Fried Chicken'.

Mary   Yes . . .?

Mike   I'm not from here.

Mary   Right . . .

Mike   No.

Mary   So . . .? Yeah I know that, Mike, I know you're not from Scotland, you're from America, I know that!

Mike   I'm not from America either.

Mary   Well, what you're *Canadian*? What are you saying?

Mike   When I say I'm not from here, I mean I'm not from here, as in I'm not from *here. Here.*

Mary   Here being . . .?

Mike   I'm not from this planet.

Mary   Right . . . ok . . . so what – what are you saying here, Mike, you're from another planet, you're an *alien*?

Mike   No I'm not an alien.

Mary   Because if you're saying you're an alien that's a pretty insane and ridiculous thing to be saying to a person, that's a bit, it's a bit, yeah, you know?

Mike   I'm not an alien.

Mary   Good! Because that's a stupid crazy *daft* thing to be saying to someone.

Mike   I'm an angel.

Mary   A what?

Mike   I'm an angel.

Mary   An angel?

Mike   Yes.

Mary   What do you mean?

Mike   I mean . . . I'm an angel.

Mary   Right. But what do you mean? I mean what do you actually mean? When you say that?

Mike   I mean that I'm an angel. I'm a celestial entity. I'm a 'divine messenger', if you will. From Heaven.

Mary   Ohhhhh . . . ok.

Mike   I know this is very hard for you to understand.

Mary   Yes I think this is hard to understand, you're right.

Mike   I know you're of a time of a . . . that this particular generation, this particular epoch, you aren't especially open to the possibility of this kind of occurrence, of what might be termed 'divine grace' or 'divine intervention'.

Mary   Hmmhmm, yeah, yeah, sure. Sure.

Mike   But this is the truth. Ok? This is the truth I'm telling you. And I'd ask you – sincerely, Mary, I'm asking you to open your mind and to open up your soul. God sent me here to speak to you specifically, Mary. To bring you the Good News. God has seen you, Mary. You are not alone. You have never been alone. God has witnessed your misery and your struggles through life. He has watched your loneliness and your despair. He has cried when you have cried. And laughed when you have laughed. And he is giving you a child, Mary. You're going to give birth to a special child, a beautiful boy. A child to bring healing to a wounded world. A world in pain, just as you yourself have been in pain for many, many years. And he'll save it, Mary. Your child will be a saviour to all mankind and to the world.

Mary   And this is the reason you've never heard of Kentucky Fried Chicken?

Mike   You don't believe me. Ok. I knew this would happen.

Mary   No, hey, no, I mean, hey, come on. It's perfectly plausible everything you're saying. I mean, why not? You know. Why not?

Mike   You're being sarcastic, I can see that.

Mary   No this is funny. This is very funny, Mike. Is your name Mike?

Mike   It's Michael.

Mary   Oh yes, Michael, that's more biblical.

Mike   My friends call me Mike.

Mary   Oh your friends? All your friends up there in Heaven? All the other angels?

Mike   I'm being serious.

Mary   And what about Jesus? Does Jesus call you Mike as well?

Mike   No. He calls me Michael.

Mary   Oh you know him then, you know Jesus, that's nice for you, you know Jesus.

Mike   Well, look, I didn't want to tell –

Mary   *Shut up!*

He shuts up.

Mary   Who do you think I am? You really do think I'm daft don't you?

Mike   I told you I don't know what that word means.

Mary   Why are you doing this? Why would you make up such an outrageous lie!

Mike   It's not a lie, I promise you.

Mary   I know I lied to you and I've . . . Look, I'm sorry if I've hurt your feelings or if I've insulted you or if I've put you in a situation that's made you feel uncomfortable. But to say *that*. To treat me like *that*. Like I'm a fool. That I'd believe such a . . .

No. Shame on you, Mike. That's disgraceful. How dare you.

Mike   I'm sorry you're hurt. But I'm telling you the truth.

Mary   That cannot be the truth!

Mike   I'm telling you, it is.

Mary   How can that be the truth? Stop insulting me! Why did you say it? Tell me why you would say such a thing!

Mike   Why don't you just go? Alright! You think I'm lying, you think I'm crazy, just go! You said you would go, you promised you'd go! So go!

Mary   I'm not going!

Mike   You promised!

Mary   You can't say something like that to me and expect me to just leave!

Mike   I knew this would happen!

Mary   I am going nowhere until you tell me why you're making up such a ridiculous lie!

Mike   Yes, I'm lying! Ok Mary, it's a lie! I'm crazy, ok? I'm a NUTBAG! Everything I just told you I made up, so why don't you just get out of here and leave me alone! Thank you! Goodbye!

Mary   No this isn't a lie.

Mike   What?

Mary   I can see you're not lying. I have a good instinct for this.

Mike   Oh God.

Mary   I mean it's clearly not true because how could it be, but you really believe it, don't you?

Mike   Yes I really believe it, because it's TRUE, that's why!

Mary   Well, you must be crazy, mustn't you? You must be insane? That's the only explanation.

Mike   Yeah yeah. Yeah yeah yeah. Can you leave now?

Mary   Why do you want me to leave?

Mike   Ok, if I tell you why I want you to leave, will you leave?

Even if you think I'm nuts will you please keep your promise and leave?

I don't care what you think of me but will you please just go when I tell you this?

Mary   Yes.

Mike   Now I'm serious this time.

Mary   Yes. Ok. Yes.

Mike   I have a limited amount of time on earth.

Forty-seven hours to be exact.

I met you at seven o'clock last night and I have to be back in Heaven by six o'clock tomorrow night British time.

Heaven is very nice and being an angel is great but being a human being for forty-seven hours is as exciting as life gets for an angel.

I like having a body. I like eating. I like kissing. I like getting drunk. I like walking. I like feeling real. Having skin and teeth and hair and . . .

He grabs at his skin. He grabs at objects around the room.

I love this! This!

But most of all I like breathing. I like sitting on a park bench, inhaling and exhaling, watching squirrels and pigeons and dogs. I like sunshine and rain and . . . weather? Isn't that what you call it? I like weather. We don't have weather in Heaven.

None of the other angels like being down here anymore. It's not the same as it used to be.

You used to revere us. You believed in us when we spoke. And now you don't. You no longer accept us unquestioningly. Which is a good thing. It shows you're evolving.

But it makes our job a lot harder. It leads to . . . well, it leads to situations like this.

When God gives us these tasks no one volunteers willingly anymore.

But I did.

Because I thought – well, to be honest, I thought, stupidly I thought, I could cheat God. I thought I could fulfil my mission, get you . . . you know . . . *filled* . . . and then not have to tell you. I mean, you'll find out some day eventually, when your baby son starts walking on water or resurrects his pet hamster, so why do I need to tell you? I don't have to be a divine messenger this time, do I? The baby is the message. That's what I was thinking.

But the thing with having God as your employer is he's always one step ahead of you. A thousand steps ahead of you. He knew I couldn't get out of here without telling you. That some part of you needed to hear it and wouldn't let me go.

I'm using my remaining time on earth to visit London. I've never been to London before. I've never been on a train before.

Last time I was on earth, I was helping Cyril and Methodius convert the Slavs. And believe me, that was a lot easier than dealing with you.

So I've told you the truth. I've delivered the Messiah into your womb and I've handed you your divine mission. Now if you'll excuse me, I have to pack and get ready. I'm booked on the ten thirty to King's Cross and I don't want to miss it. I have tickets for *The Lion King.*

He starts packing a small suitcase.

Mary   Well, I don't believe a word of what you're saying. Obviously what you're saying is ridiculous.

But let's say, for sake of argument, let's say it's true.

Mike   It is true.

Mary   Let's say it is.

Why me?

Mike   Uh-huh.

Mary   Why would –

Mike   Hmhmm.

Mary   Why would God – not that there is a God –

Mike   There is.

Mary   For sake of argument, let's say that there is.

Mike   There is.

Mary   Yes for sake of argument. If there was a God, why would He choose me? I'm not a virgin!

Mike   Yes, He's aware of that.

Mary   So why would God choose me?

Mike   You think you're the first human being in history tasked with a divine purpose who asks, 'Why me?' Have you even read the Bible? What do you think Abraham said? What about Moses?

No one but God knows why God chooses the ones He chooses. I don't know why He chose you. You can ask Him yourself after you die. Have you seen my pants?

Mary   There, they are there.

Mike   Thanks.

Mary   No. None of this makes sense. This is madness! This is not true. None of this can be true!

He finishes packing.

Mike   But you know it is. Don't you? Deep down, somewhere buried inside you, you sense that this is true?

Mary   So when we made love last night –

Mike   We didn't make love.

Mary   Yes we did.

Mike   We didn't make love.

Mary   But I remember

Mike   We didn't. It's not permitted. The last time angels made love to humans it led to the flood. You know about Noah right?

Mary   Aye the big boat and the animals. Two by two. I remember learning about it in Sunday school.

Mike   Yeah the same day Jenny O'Hara stole your favourite colouring pencil? The big red one?

Mary   Ohhhh she was a right wee bitch, Jenny O'Ha – hang on, how do you know about that? Are you a pal of Jenny's? Is this revenge?

Mike   No, I did my research before coming here. And you really need to forgive her for that. You held that grudge all the way to high school and stole her first boyfriend from her? Darren *McCartney*, right?

Mary   You can't . . . you must have been – how –

Mike   But the flood? The flood was hell on earth. When I think back to that time I still get chills. God promised he'd never do anything like that again. So any angel who even tries to make love to a human, there are consequences I can't even tell you about, Mary. A chaste kiss is allowed in certain circumstances but that's as far as it goes.

Mary   No this is – we did, Mike. I know you're lying because I remember! I remember the sex!

Mike   Listen to me. God is a perfect gentleman. And we're encouraged – more than encouraged – to behave the same way.

Mary   But –

Mike   You had a little too much to drink. (You are from Glasgow, after all.) I put you to bed. We lay together. I held you all through the night until the sun came up. What you remember was a feeling in your dreams. That's why you woke up and thought, 'och aye the noo, I've never felt this way before.'

The Lord came to meet you with his perfect love.

I need to get ready.

Mary   Why are you American?

Mike   Can you turn around please?

Mary   Oh. Sorry.

She turns around. He starts getting changed.

If God sent you here, why couldn't he have made you Scottish?

Mike   We're created to reflect the appearance of the group that makes up the dominant empire on earth at the time. And as far as I'm aware, Scotland is not the dominant empire on earth.

Mary   No it's not.

Mike   In previous epochs, it made things easier. When people had more deference for the powerful. Had you met me two thousand years ago, I would have been a Roman.

Mary   I see.

Mike   In the 1800s I was English.

Mary   Ugh that's a shame for you.

Mike   Yeah and he doesn't appreciate your xenophobia.

Mary   It is not xenophobic to make jokes about the English. It's my birthright as a Glaswegian. You tell him I said that.

Mike   I'm not finding it helpful this time round though, being American. Since I got here, everyone's been really rude to me.

Mary   Och, that's just Edinburgh folk. He should have sent you directly to Glasgow. We're much friendlier there.

Mike   That's not what He said. He thought I'd have an easier time in Edinburgh.

Mary   Even during the Festival?

Mike   God loves the Edinburgh Festival.

Mary   Does he?

Mike   He loves festivals of any kind. He loves it when people get together and celebrate things. He thinks you don't do it enough.

He checks his watch.

It's . . . ahm . . .

Mary   Aye.

He walks to the door.

You know I don't believe you? You know that don't you?

Mike   It doesn't matter if you believe me or not. You'll see it when your baby is born. You'll look into his eyes and see his beauty, his tenderness, his divinity. You'll see.

He starts to leave.

Mary   So am I the same Mary as the Mary from the Bible?

Mike   No. How could you be? You're different people.

Mary   Like a reincarnation?

Mike   No there's no such thing as – (*He sighs, frustrated, and checks his watch.*)

The original Mary's in heaven.

Mary   What's she like?

Mike   Oh she's lovely. She's so kind and gentle and sweet. And she buys the best Christmas presents.

Mary   See, I'm nothing like that. Are you sure you've got the right person? I'm not kind or gentle or sweet. I'm bad-tempered, I'm lazy, I'm selfish, I'm jealous, I don't have a husband, I buy awful Christmas presents. I am very very *very* imperfect! I can't raise the Son of God, especially not on my own.

Mike   The last time he came as a lamb. But now he's returning as a lion. So maybe he needs a more ferocious mother this time round.

And you're not on your own, Mary.

You were never on your own.

He is about to leave but stops himself. He turns around.

Can I kiss you?

Mary   Ahm . . . sure . . .

Mike   It might be another thousand years before I kiss a woman again.

I know you think I'm . . . *daft* . . . but . . .

I want to remember you.

He steps forward and kisses her tenderly on the lips.

He then breaks away and exits abruptly.

Mary *sits down at the end of the bed. She shakes her head in disbelief. She looks down at her belly. She feels her belly.*

The opening of The Lion King *plays.*

End.

Discover. Read. Listen. Watch.

A NEW WAY TO ENGAGE WITH PLAYS

This award-winning digital library features over 3,000 playtexts, 400 audio plays, 300 hours of video and 360 scholarly books.

Playtexts published by Methuen Drama, The Arden Shakespeare, Faber & Faber, Playwrights Canada Press, Aurora Metro Books and Nick Hern Books.

Audio Plays from L.A. Theatre Works featuring classic and modern works from the oeuvres of leading American playwrights.

Video collections including films of live performances from the RSC, The Globe and The National Theatre, as well as acting masterclasses and BBC feature films and documentaries.

FIND OUT MORE:
www.dramaonlinelibrary.com • @dramaonlinelib

Methuen Drama Modern Plays

include

Bola Agbaje
Ayad Akhtar
Edward Albee
Jean Anouilh
John Arden
Peter Barnes
Clare Barron
Sebastian Barry
Alistair Beaton
Brendan Behan
Edward Bond
William Boyd
Bertolt Brecht
Howard Brenton
Amelia Bullmore
Anthony Burgess
Leo Butler
Jim Cartwright
Lolita Chakrabarti
Caryl Churchill
Lucinda Coxon
Tim Crouch
Shelagh Delaney
Ishy Din
Claire Dowie
David Edgar
David Eldridge
Dario Fo
Michael Frayn
John Godber
James Graham
David Greig
John Guare
Lauren Gunderson
Peter Handke
David Harrower
Jonathan Harvey
Robert Holman
David Ireland
Sarah Kane

Barrie Keeffe
Jasmine Lee-Jones
Anders Lustgarten
Duncan Macmillan
David Mamet
Patrick Marber
Martin McDonagh
Alistair McDowall
Arthur Miller
Tom Murphy
Phyllis Nagy
Anthony Neilson
Peter Nichols
Ben Okri
Joe Orton
Vinay Patel
Joe Penhall
Luigi Pirandello
Stephen Poliakoff
Lucy Prebble
Peter Quilter
Mark Ravenhill
Philip Ridley
Willy Russell
Sam Shepard
Martin Sherman
Chris Shinn
Jackie Sibblies Drury
Wole Soyinka
Simon Stephens
Kae Tempest
Laura Wade
Anne Washburn
Timberlake Wertenbaker
Roy Williams
Snoo Wilson
Theatre Workshop
Frances Ya-Chu Cowhig
Benjamin Zephaniah

For a complete listing of
Methuen Drama titles, visit:
www.bloomsbury.com/drama

Follow us on X and keep up to date with
our news and publications
@MethuenDrama